Dedicated to Monica

PIRATE

After reading a book about pirates...
A pirate ship moved inside of me.
The deck has crew members running around!
Such fun when we sail out to sea!

The book I read was about boy pirates...
I'd never heard of a girl pirate before.
The pirate ship inside of me has an all-girl crew...
So, I definitely want to learn more!

The commander of the pirate ship -
Gives the all-girl crew plenty to do!
The only boy on the crew is the chef...
Otherwise, girl pirates do everything boy pirates do!

On the high seas the pirate ship sails...
Bouncing up and down rapidly...
I hope to get over my seasickness soon!
Otherwise being a pirate might not be meant for me!

MEERKAT

It's pretty cool when meerkats...
Raise their pups inside of me.
I have to stock up on veggies...
They love to eat them for their tea!

PATTERN

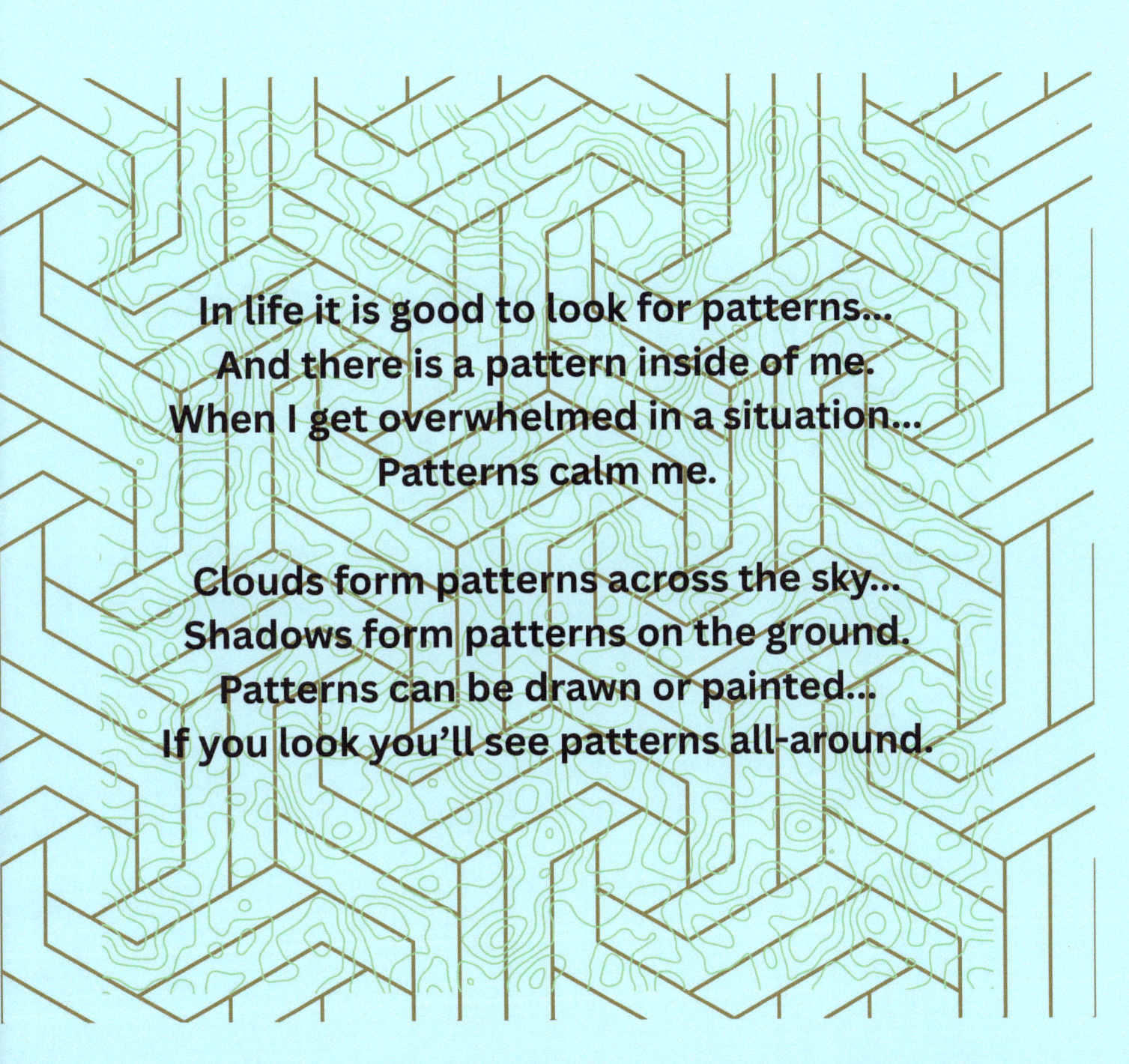

In life it is good to look for patterns...
And there is a pattern inside of me.
When I get overwhelmed in a situation...
Patterns calm me.

Clouds form patterns across the sky...
Shadows form patterns on the ground.
Patterns can be drawn or painted...
If you look you'll see patterns all-around.

At the beach I find a pattern in the sand.
The tide comes in, and washes it out to sea.
But I don't worry, I can always find new patterns...
And for backup I have a pattern inside of me.

DICTIONARY

I'm an excellent speller...
There's a dictionary inside of me.
I read it from cover to cover...
To expand my vocabulary.

I learn a new word every single day.
I recite the words to memory.
I say them out loud. Then I spell them out loud.
Then I'm ready for the next Spelling B!

THESAURUS

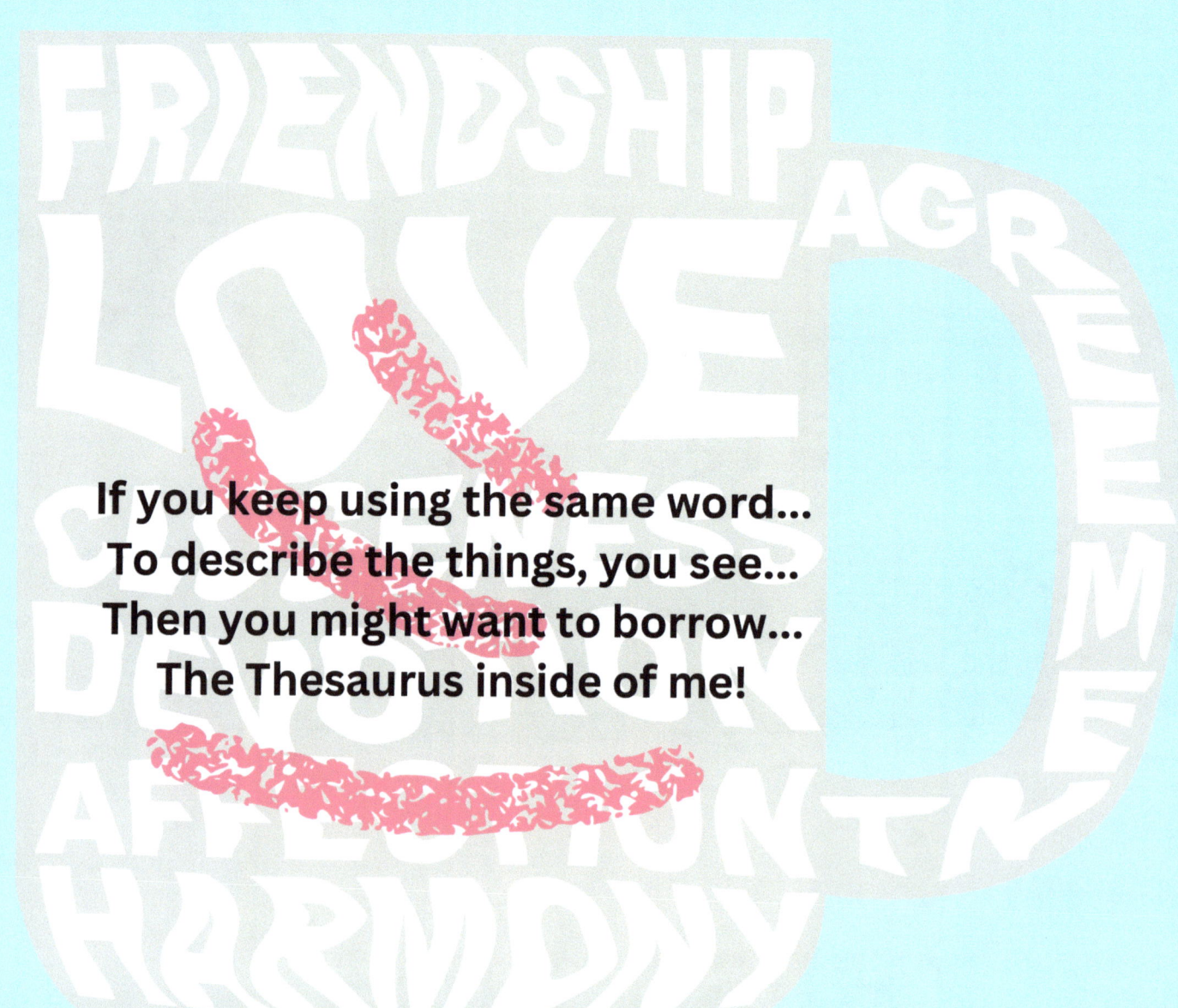

If you keep using the same word...
To describe the things, you see...
Then you might want to borrow...
The Thesaurus inside of me!

UNIVERSE

All things need a hug...
There's a universe inside of me.
I close my arms and hug the universe...
And in return the universe hugs me!

PATHWAYS

On the road of life, we can choose which way to go...
There are pathways inside of me.
When I'm afraid to choose which path to take...
I remain stationary.

Daddy says half the fun is choosing a path...
That I shouldn't worry whether its wrong or right.
Either way, I'll be learning something new...
Either way I'll gain new incite.

But I don't want to waste a pathway!
If I choose to take one too early....
Will that pathway wither up?
Will it no longer be available to me?

Daddy tells me not to over-think...
Which is something I do naturally.
I like to think before I try new things...
There's plenty of time to choose for me!

KINDNESS

ALWAYS CHOOSE KINDNESS

Kindness is a choice...
And there's kindness inside of me.
Kindness lives...
Inside of everybody.

When I choose to be kind...
It brings out the best in me.
When you decide to be kind...
Your kindness helps everybody.

Be kind.
Like me.
Be kind.
To everybody.

FREE WILL

My sister always gets straight A's...
And wins all kinds of trophies.
I wanted to throw them into the garbage...
Then Free Will moved inside of me.

"You could do that," Free Will explained.
"But there will be consequences if you do."
"What do you mean?" I asked.
Free Will said, "How would you feel if your sister
did that to you?"

GREAT CHOICE

At first I didn't answer...
I was putting myself in her shoes.
Doing that made my tummy hurt...
And the hurt gave me some clues.

Free Will said, "That's the power of Free Will...
"You can choose what to do.
"Go ahead. Choose whatever you want to...
"The choice is up to you."

I didn't throw my sister's trophies in the bin...
Thanks to the Free Will inside of me.
Instead, I decided to work very hard...
And earn my very own trophies!

SNAPDRAGON

I wished for a dragon for my birthday.
Now there's a Snapdragon inside of me!
The Birthday Wish Fairy...
Really messed things up for me!

A Snapdragon is a flower...
It is pretty and one to admire.
But it would even be better...
If it could breathe fire!

CLOWNFISH

I'm afraid of clowns...
Or I used to be...
That's when a Clownfish...
Moved inside of me.

The ocean is now my tummy...
And although the Clownfish inside of me...
Has the word "clown" in his name...
I'm not scared because I think he is funny!

SKUNK

I decided not to shower anymore...
Now a skunk lives inside of me.
Mom and Dad used to say I smelled bad before...
But now they plug their noses when they see me!

At school, the other kids laugh and point...
One calls me "Molly-le-peu."
In revenge the skunk in me let go a big stink...
I couldn't stop laughing! Could you?

The Principal made me sit in the hall...
While we waited for my parents to arrive.
I had company...the skunk inside of me...
We buzzed like two bees in a hive!

Dad, Mom, and I left the school...
They weren't angry with me.
Each took a hold of one of my hands...
And we walked out of the school we three.

At the bus stop the driver opened the door...
The skunk inside me set a spray free...
The driver slammed the door and drove away...
We decided to walk home as a family.

COLOUR WHEEL

Colouring can be a lot of fun!
Or more complicated than need be.
Which is what happened when...
A Colour Wheel moved inside of me.

Before I just grabbed a crayon...
Any colour straight out of the pack...
Then I'd colour something...
And put the crayon back.

Now there's a lot of choosing to do...
To decide what colour blends well with what I see.
Life is sure more complicated since...
A colour wheel moved inside of me.

ELBOWS UP

I heard the P.M. say, "Elbow's up!"
Then a hockey match began inside of me.
I prefer to watch hockey live...
Even when it is on t.v.!

It was the Canadien's vs the Leaf's...
Both teams played equally.
I hope to have a career in hockey one day...
Maybe I'll drive a zamboni!

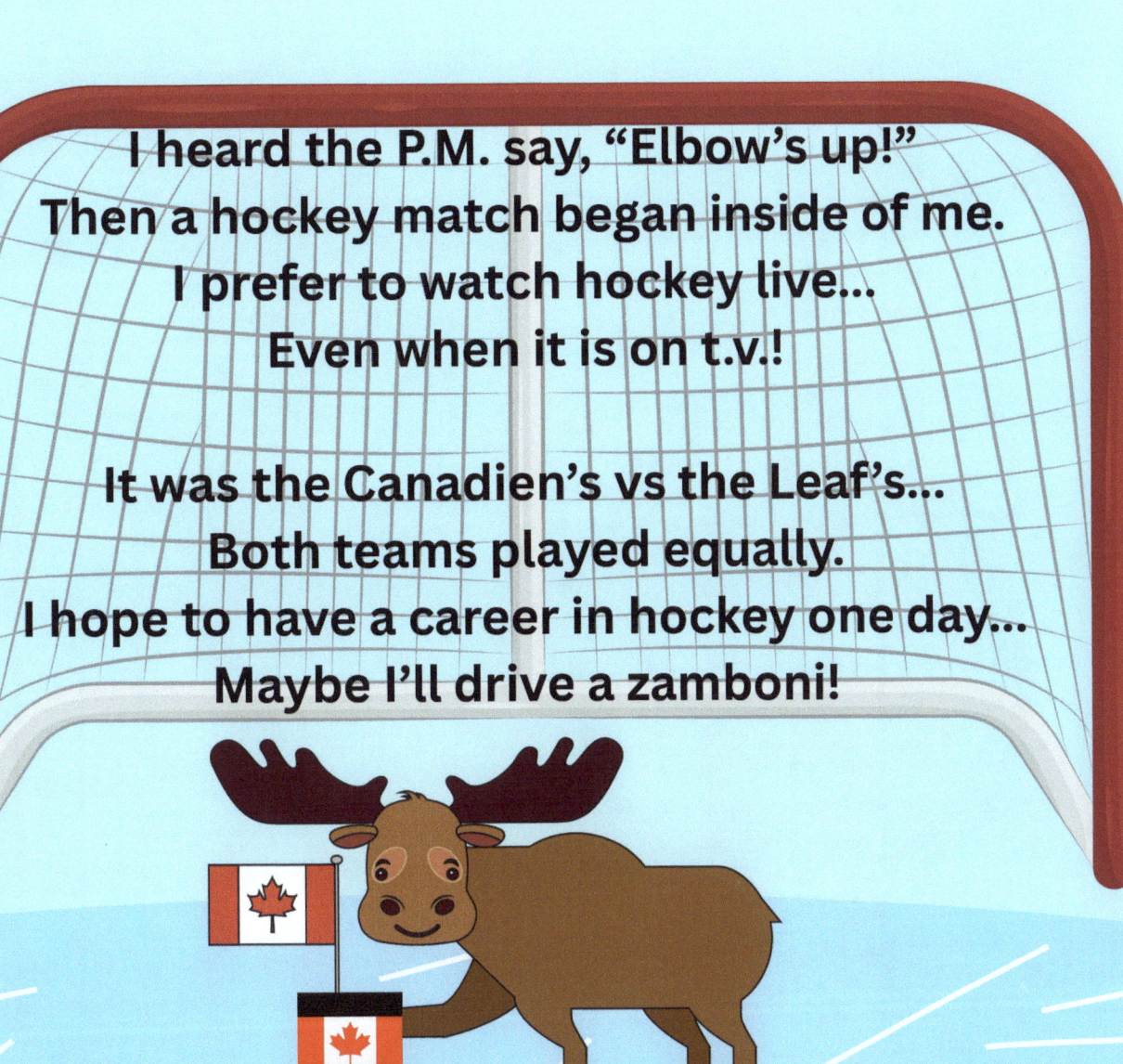

ROLLERCOASTER

I don't need to go to the amusement park anymore...
Since a rollercoaster moved inside of me.
Now life is much more exciting!
Than sitting around looking lazy.

I can choose any rollercoaster car...
I prefer one right at the back.
Because it gives me more time...
To finish eating my snack!

Although screaming on my own...
Isn't as much fun to do!
But you soon get over your fear of heights!
When there's a rollercoaster inside of you!

WOODPECKER

It's a rat-a-tat-tat all day long!
Since a woodpecker moved inside of me.
"Doesn't all that pecking give you a headache?" I ask.
The woodpecker is pecking too loud to hear me!

I get into my pajamas...
I pull up the covers and turn off the light with glee!
Because the woodpecker is now sleeping...
And it's peaceful inside of me.

CARIBOU

Ever wondered what you would do?
If a caribou moved inside of you?
I can tell you about it personally...
Since a caribou moved inside of me.

The caribou doesn't make much noise...
Or cause all kinds of commotion.
But he misses his family...
And I can sense his emotions.

I ask him to tell me where they are.
He says he can show me.
But it's far away - too far to walk...
And I'm not old enough to drive you see.

He says flying would be quicker...
He's from Alberta, Calgary.
Dad and I arrange it with the airline...
And we return the caribou to his family.

SPACESHIP

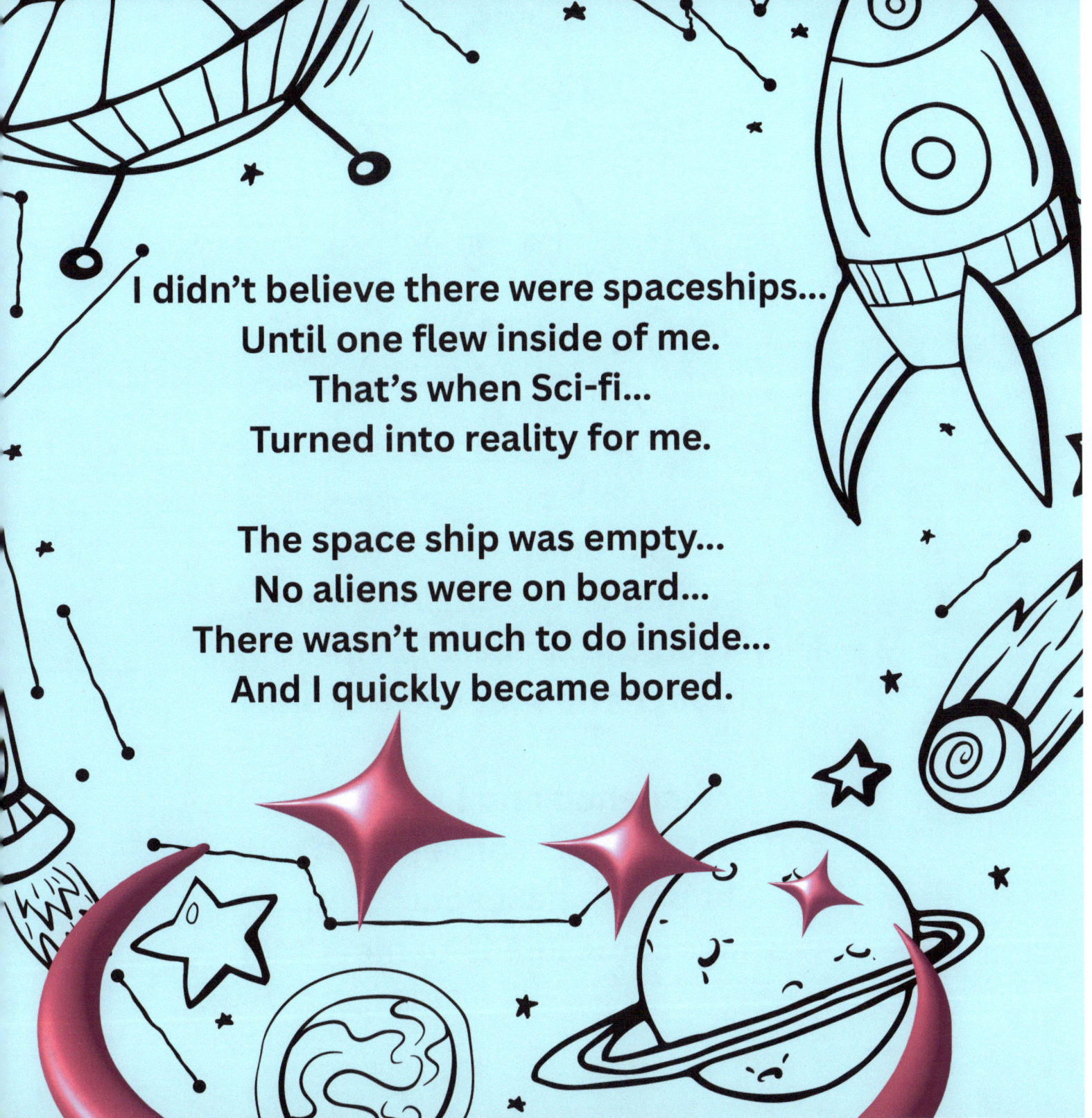

I didn't believe there were spaceships...
Until one flew inside of me.
That's when Sci-fi...
Turned into reality for me.

The space ship was empty...
No aliens were on board...
There wasn't much to do inside...
And I quickly became bored.

I sat on the bridge...
I listened to the engines hum...
Then I felt the spaceship vibrating...
Through the seat like a drum!

I laughed and I roared!
Then the spaceship ejected me!
I hope the next spaceship...
Brings some aliens to meet me!

FRIZZLED AND FRAZZLED

Some mornings I can't get it together.
There's a frizzle and frazzle in me!
When I feel like hiding under the covers...
And know that hiding, isn't like me!

Which is why I named what I was feeling...
I say, "Oh, this is a Frizzled and Frazzled Day!"
I laugh when I say it,
Knowing that it will soon go away!

I get showered and dressed...
I go down to eat breakfast...
Doing normal things lifts my spirits...
I know the frizzle and frazzle won't last.

Having friends and family around helps me...
Conquer the frizzle and frazzle in me.
I listen to music, I paint - do things I love...
Until the Frizzled and Frazzled Day leaves me!

EAVESDROPPER

It can be fun to be an eavesdropper...
I didn't know until one moved inside of me.
Sometimes I stand in the hall and listen...
To what others are saying about me.

The conversations can be quite funny...
Often times about silly kinds of things...
Once in awhile you over hear personal things...
Like my brother gave his girlfriend a ring.

The hard part about being an eavesdropper is...
When you hear juicy bits you want to share!
But what you heard wasn't meant for you...
And you really shouldn't have been there.

So, I think I want to get earplugs...
For the eavesdropper inside of me.
Being an eavesdropper isn't...
The kind of person I want to be!

HAIKU

**FIRE FARTING DRAGON
IS LIVING INSIDE OF ME:
A TWO-PRONGED ATTACK.**

Write a Haiku

Colour a Snapdragon

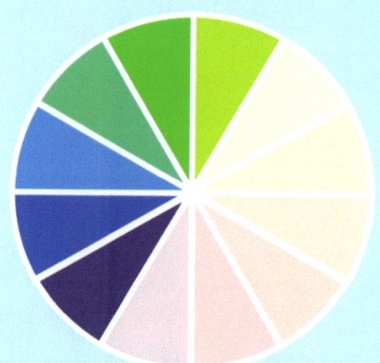

Write a Poem or Story

ALSO BY CATHY MCGOUGH

POETRY SERIES:

There's a Chimpanzee Inside of Me!
There's a Jumping Bean Inside of Me!
There's a Reindeer Inside of Me!
There's a Hero inside of Me!
"There's a Panda inside of Me!"
"There's a Mock Turtle inside of Me!"

JUMP SERIES:

Jump Like a Caribou!
Jump Like a Kangaroo!
Jump at the Zoo!
Jump and Say P.U.!
Jump and Say Boo!
Jump and Say Valentine's Day Is
For Kids Too!
Jump and Look For a Clue!
Jump and Say Happy Birthday to You!
Jump For Everything Blue!
Jump, Hop and Say Happy Easter To You!
Jump and Say Cock-A-Doodle-Do!
Jump and Sing Da-Do-Do-Do!
Jump and Ask Who? Who?
Jump and Squawk Like a Cockatoo!
Jump and Ask Is It You or Ewe?
Jump and Say There's an Ewww in My Stew!
Jump and Say Merry Christmas To You!
Jump and Cheer Happy New Year!
Jump and Say There's a Moo-Moo in a Tutu!
Jump and Say There's a Hare in My Hair!
Jump and Say My Aunt Ate An Ant!
Jump and Say There's An Aardvark
In The Amusement Park!
Jump and Roar For The Dinosaurs!
Jump and Buzz Like A Bee!
Jump and Flutter Like A Butterfly!
Jump and Pop Like Popcorn!
Jump and Ribbit Like A Frog!
Jump and Snore Like A Koala!

Jump and Snuffle Like A Platypus!
Jump and Grunt Like A Groundhog!
Jump and Say Hello!
Jump and Say Friend!
Jump and Say Peace!
Jump and Say Sky!
Jump and Say Merry Christmas!
Jump and Say Happy New Year!
Jump and Say Fun!
Jump and Say Family!
Jump and Say Jump!

CLAP FOR SERIES:

Clap for 1!
Clap for 2!
Clap for 3!
Clap for 4!
Clap for 5!
Clap for 6!
Clap for 7!
Clap for 8!
Clap for 9!
Clap for 10!

The Cat Who Said Hello
The Three Boulders
Billy Shakespeare
Billie Shakespeare
Learn To Draw With Symmetry
ABC More Learn to Draw With Symmetry

Non-Fiction
103 Fundraising Ideas For Parent Volunteers With Schools and Teams